I0477739

Table of Contents

Introduction 4

    If you are reading this, you could be… 6

    Why Should You Earn Extra Money 11

    To Freelance or not to Freelance....................................... 13

    Find that spare time 15

STEP 1 - Making an inventory of your skills 19

    Skill List 23

    Browse other freelancers 24

STEP 2 - Finding Your Niche Market 26

    What is a niche? 26

    Why do market research? 27

    What are the things to look out for? 28

    Where can I search? 29

Step 3 - The Profile That Gets You Hired................................. 31

    Remember natural lights 32

    Pick the right angle 33

    Consider your clothing.. 34

    Put relevant skills on profile 38

    Write a description that never gets ignored........................ 39

    Setting up your pricing and rate 42

    Taking Relevant Tests 44

    Building a portfolio 46

STEP 4 - Writing Proposals and Selling Yourself....................... 49

    Techniques to win Contracts 50

STEP 5 - Keeping the Wheels Turning..................................... 53

    How to attract high paying clients..................................... 55

    Under-promising and Over-delivering 57

Conclusion 59

Introduction

In the year 1991, the World Wide Web went live to the world. There was no Facebook live, twitter reporters and there was not even bloggers or vloggers to do press release to let everyone know. In fact, most people around the world didn't even know what the Internet was. Now it does not really matter who was the person or persons we should thank for this great gift of technology. All we know is that we are enjoying it nowadays in more than a million ways we never thought possible.

Let us now define the word "freelance." It turns out that this word is way too old compared to all of us. Heck, it is even older than the word "internet." It turns out, that our grandparents could have been freelancers in the past as well. The dictionary defines freelance as working for different companies at different times rather than being permanently employed by one company.

Of course it never happened overnight that both of these terms came out and then online freelancing was born. Because as the internet became a part of our daily lives, the concept of freelance work online found its way into the internet. With the convenience brought by technology, people began looking for clients and work to finish projects even without the need to be physically collaborating, hence the term freelancing became synonymous to "working remotely."

With the unimaginable growth of the internet and the ever-evolving technology, this is actually the best time to get started with having an online career. And if you haven't already, I will give you a few short reasons why you should try it.

- You develop new skills and expertise by working with various clients
- You have more flexibility with time and freedom in terms of location
- You can build a network of contacts from around the globe
- You can find a full-time gig with these contacts
- You earn extra source of money

I have put together in this book the things I have learned from my traditional jobs and freelancing career as a graphic/web designer. I have compiled in this book the things that I have tried and tested and I am sharing with you the things you need to do so you will be aware of the things that you shouldn't. I have included actionable tips and suggestions for you to get started.

The techniques and tips might not specifically work for each type of job out there but the ideas I've put down in here will help you find clients, enable you to raise your value as a freelancer and help you be more productive with better efficiency so you can have more time for yourself or family. If you are someone who wishes to try this but do not know where to start, I encourage you to read on and take action. Words of tough love: None of these would be useful in the end if you do not act.

If you are already doing your freelancing career and you think you are doing great, well I am happy for you. I would still want you to hear bits and pieces of my story and I do hope I can share with you insights that could be very useful in some aspects of career and dealing with clients.

Majority of the examples I will mention here are specifically for Upwork, because currently, Upwork is the leading platform from all of the freelancing websites out there. But do not worry, as these concepts are all very applicable with the others. They all have almost the same framework.

So take your cup of coffee or tea, get a pen and paper if you'd like taking notes, and turn that page.

If you are reading this, you could be…

An employee.

I am going to respectfully assume you're getting tired of your repetitive, tedious routine every day. Yes, you have a job that pays the bills and gives you all the basic needs, but you sometimes feel like a living zombie working for that pay slip. And you are contemplating if it is really possible to work remotely. Online freelancing is just one way to do it. You can actually try taking small steps outside your comfort zone. You are here now because you want to give it a shot and see what other opportunities might there be, in the four corners of your monitor. You could be bored, and you want to breakout from the monotonous and bland happenings of your everyday life.

I get that you do not want to spend too much time working, because hey, you have a life to live and this should not take too much of your time, yes? Damn right, because that is what part-time jobs are for. In the older times, to get a part-time job, you have to literally wear different hats, change uniforms and be at different places so you can go to work.

Nobody can deny that it is hard—having two, or three different jobs. It's hard to imagine juggling different sets of responsibilities. At the end of the day, the extra money is your motivator to keep going, but it will be harder if you're trying to ignore burnout and stress. Everyone wants to earn more, right? But even if you have your daytime job, or a fulltime job where you get your steady cash flow—sometimes it is just not enough.

Just curious.

There could be a lot of reasons why you need to consider working from home.

- You could be a stay-at-home mom because you need to take care of your kid.
- You could be a former employee who just lost his job.

- You want to do something productive on your free time. (Which rarely happens!)

Actually, you just need a few things to get the wheels turning—a stable internet connection, a computer, and you. That is it. That is all you need to start freelancing.

Believe it or not, freelancing offers a lot on the table when it comes to flexibility. You can literally work anywhere as long as you have a stable internet and a computer. It does not really matter which tool you use although some jobs can be done using a mobile phone or a tablet. You just need to have the tools. It all depends on your resourcefulness. The number of hours you want to spend doing it is really up to you, and you can choose when you want to do it. How cool is that for night owls and non-morning people?

You literally do not have a boss—but you have clients. It doesn't require you to commute or drive to work. You can work in your pajamas. You can work on the couch, bedroom or dining area. It is a different story though if you need to dress up for an interview or a meeting. These are just some of the things that you will care less about when you start doing freelancing.

Compared to the past generations, workers have no choice but to burn those 8+ hours in the office. Some people even bring jobs at home. Some people even need to leave their homes for work abroad, which is a tough choice. Technology lifted off that burden on us. It gives us more choices. Back then the choices are very limited—not anymore.

Looking for extra income.

Is freelancing is a good source of steady income? For beginners, it is a challenge to get the first client but when you do have 3-5 regularly paying clients, it is sustainable.

Right now I want to be brutally honest with you. It is not stable. I usually charge $10 to $20 for small projects that I can finish within an hour. On some days I can close a deal with a $250 book design where I can complete a draft within 2 hours. There are days that I have to reject interviews for new projects because I've got more than enough on my plate. It is not stable because there is no limit to what you can earn within a month, as compared to an employee that gets the same amount each payday.

Don't get me wrong, I am not saying this is a very easy thing to do. It is not. It only gets easier if you already know the important elements when you hunt for a job. And if you are properly equipped in the profile department, you can be sure that getting the remote job that favors you in many ways will be worth the effort.

You think freelancing is competitive?

Truth is, whenever there is a healthy competition, it just means there is money on it. This applies in the industry of selling as well. Have you ever wondered why there are a lot of fitness gurus that claims they are the best? When you get to a bookstore and see lots and lots of books that are best-selling, what are they about? Right. Fitness. Now do you really think it is saturated? No. There is definitely money on it and people are willing to pay for it. Because if there is no competition at all—man, you should start worrying. Upwork for example has about twelve million freelancers and five million clients that are paying to get their jobs done. Now that is approximately about one client to two freelancer ratio. If you think you can be one of the best out there, and you can outdo others, then don't overthink it.

There are a lot of freelancing sites available as of now so you should not worry if there is saturation. It just happened that Upwork is at the top of the game that is why majority of the clients choose it. Now heads up, it's a big, big world out there. There are a lot of platforms to choose from. Do not think as if it's the end of the world if your profile gets unapproved, or rejected. Find another place to grow. Improve your craft, work on yourself to the point that you become so good at what you do and clients cannot ignore you anymore.

Begin with the end in mind.

It's always a good feeling when you have that extra cash that you do not need to take away from the monthly budget. Maybe book that trip that you've always wanted, buy that shoes that you always stare at the mall, or spend the weekend with your kids in a nearby theme park while splurging huge amounts on eating out. Yes it is time that is most valuable. Yes it is your presence that counts. But let's face it—your extra money can buy you happiness. That is the truth—money is a great motivator. The things you like, the activities you want to do—money enables it.

Look, I am not saying you should leave employment. I'm here to tell you that you can earn extra money on the side by choosing to spend your free time on something productive. I'm not saying that you sacrifice your time with family or put away your hobbies because we do not want that. I am not saying you set aside your "me-time" or give up an hour or two to get some headspace to recuperate, like, playing a video game or having a basketball match with friends. We all need time to escape reality because it refuels us. It is just a matter of choice to decide which matters to you most.

If you're really serious about this, here's what you can do. Set aside one or two hours each day for just doing things related to your freelance project and start committing yourself to it. Go to a room where no one disturbs you. Disable all distractions temporarily. No phone calls, no mobile games, no Facebook. Just dedicate those hours each day to it. Find and discover what type of service you can do and in the following chapters, I will share with you tips that you can apply not just on Upwork, but on every platform you can start working with. You can even apply it outside any freelancing platform. No need for you to go through trials and errors. We are going to set our sights on quick small wins. Find your niche. Serve clients and get paid.

Now to clarify things and help you do the mind setting: The reason you are holding this book right now is simple—earn extra money on the side, online. But be informed, there is no get-rich-quick scheme here, nor any hint about network marketing. There is no shortcut to succeed on this, but I can teach you everything I know about it so you can be on the right path. It does not matter whether you're choosing to do this full-time or not. Again: Find your niche. Serve clients and get paid.

Why Should You Earn Extra Money

I am very certain that most financial advice you hear has already been discussed by a lot of experts, and it surely sounds like a broken record. You have probably heard things like learning how to cut costs, and how to optimize our spending. But we hadn't really yet learned how to earn more. Hypothetically there are a lot of ways to earn more, but on this book, we will discuss only one thing—converting your skills into money with just a few hours a day.

If you cannot really go into business already because you are undecided on what business to do or what money-making methods to try, starting with this business model is the way to go, because you do not really need much capital as opposed to trying out a new business or investing money on something that can create profits. Because in the end, to become rich, you have to earn more money. My dad told me a long time ago, "You cannot save your way to being rich." You cannot out-frugal your way to being rich. Eventually, you will have to earn more money.

If you think about it, savings is not enough. This is very true if you have a budget to follow strictly. You cannot be really sure that you can keep higher amounts for savings or pay your debts. Many instances will come where you will have surprise expenses or worse—an emergency. This is why you need to keep a certain amount of cash each month as your emergency fund. Earning extra money on the side makes it easier for you to do that. Having an extra amount that you kept will help a lot when rainy days come. If you're just able to make ends meet and then keep the remaining in savings, you could pull it off but just saving money is not enough. Let's look deeper on why you should choose to earn more than cut costs. Because let's face it, why settle with being frugal if you can earn more?

With your limited amount of money coming in, there is always a limit to cutting costs. Luckily, there is no limit whatsoever to earning in freelancing. It all starts with your mindset, on how you perceive money making, and money management. More often than not, it is your history on how you were brought up that dictates how you handle your money, and so the same goes with how you think about money.

With our current economy there's obviously nothing wrong with being careful with how you spend your cash but all too often people confuse frugality with being cheap.

Given any circumstances and regardless of being responsible or not in handling money, earning more will always beat saving more.

To Freelance or not to Freelance

So is it wiser to do work for yourself as a freelancer or to work for a company that offers health care benefits and incentives? If you are on the crossroads and the thought of leaving your company both thrills and terrifies you I suggest do not rush things. There is a safer way to do this. There is a way to have that security and peace of mind when you wish to jump in and try freelancing.

There are many successful freelancers that have actually taken their skills, quit their full-time jobs and have gone full time on the stuff that they do. But before that, let me talk to you about the issues because you can actually make more money working for yourself sometimes but there's a trade-off in security and there's a lot of things to consider.

Here is how I see things on my end. If you work for no one but yourself, you often have the potential financially to make far more than you could ever make working at a full-time job. You can also hire other people, and you can scale things out. As you learn more, you can do that through freelancing. Those who are already at the top of their game raised their rates from low numbers like ten dollars an hour to high numbers like thirty dollars an hour, and many of them have also gone from decent numbers like twenty-five dollars an hour to nearly a hundred dollars an hour. It is not typical for most freelancers, but I'm telling you, it happens. Potential for growth is massive.

Working for a company on the other hand, you have more security but there's a basic limit to how much you can make and those numbers are very gradual in terms of growth. Promotions and salary increase would take years to achieve and you need to give justice to it. "To whom much is given, much will be required." Yep, that is definitely true.

Here's what I would suggest for you to do. Actually, I'd love to encourage you to stay at your full-time job and do two things in the meantime. Do the freelancing on the side so you have more money to save each month. If you're raising your income though, remind yourself not to raise your expenses because—that is counter-productive.

Put away as much money as you can in a savings account. Try to give yourself at least twelve months of emergency funds because if you start off full time freelancing and you do not get one or a couple of clients—that is one huge problem. For now, keep your full-time job but find time for activities that produce money on the side. Start doing freelancing on the side five to ten hours a week.

An ideal scenario is that if you decide to leave your job, you already have at least three to five paying clients—ideally ten. That way you don't jump out of your job and into this cold, harsh world that says like "OMG, there's no way for you to make money!"

You already have people that are paying you. You know you have value, so that is a way to really mitigate risk. You are continuing to get the security of your job. You are funneling tons of cash away into your savings account. You are also working on getting clients and there are tons of free material out there as to how to do that.

By the time you get five to ten paying clients, you can decide, "Hey am I ready to do this full-time!" There is no other better and safer way to do this and I hope it is something you'll consider for yourself as well.

Find that spare time

Isn't it interesting that I could give you a series of tactics right now and you would feel great? Yet two weeks from now, your productivity would be measurably at the exact same place that it is now.

The fact of the matter is, is that if it were simply a tactical issue then you would have already done it. You would have read a book like, "Getting Things Done" by David Allen. Or you could try a variety of other methods that have been tried to be implemented by thousands of people. The thing is, it is not simply just a tactical issue, there is far more things that are going on in our minds when it comes to productivity.

With that said, I am going to suggest three principles that you can use to double productivity. Remember, first of all, it is possible. Because there are people who are way more productive than many of us and they do a massive amount of work in the same amount of time as we have.

So here it goes. I'm going to suggest a framework for how you can get to that level of productivity as well. We all have the same amount of hours given each day so there is no reason for you to tell me that it cannot be done.

How to double your productivity

Be brutally honest with yourself. Have you heard this line before, "I'm going to do that in the morning," and then we wake up in the morning and then we find out that we are horribly unproductive. Personally, I am training myself to become a morning person. So I usually go not later than 11PM for bedtime.

If I say to myself like, "Oh I need to do some more projects tonight. Let me do it after I have dinner," You know what? I can't. Nothing's coming out. I cannot produce any great output after about 5PM. I just do not have it in my head. So now you see that there is no point in promising to yourself that you are going to do it. What I will do, is go to sleep, wake up in the morning and I'll be much better when I get back to it.

Sound familiar? How many of us go through our entire lives basically lying to ourselves? Refusing to acknowledge the way we actually are. Instead we say things like, "Yeah I really should wake up earlier." Why? If you're not a morning person, focus your productivity on where you are being really productive. Being brutally honest requires us to often acknowledge things that we do not like. So I would say be brutally honest with yourself. Ask yourself now, are you more productive in the morning or at night? Are you more productive working at a coffee shop, your office or at home?

How can you be brutally honest with yourself and determine which works or not? That brings us to my second point. Test your theory.

Test your theory.

I could give you a tactic right now. I could say TOT [The One Thing, a book by Gary Keller and Jay Papasan] is great. And TOT is a very effective approach. You can pick that up and read it from cover to cover. But if you don't do anything about it, then you'll never find out if it really works for you or not. What I have found to be highly productive is understanding different systems and then testing them rigorously. For example, one of the things I use to test was how to wake up earlier.

Recently I've been testing how to go to bed earlier and and I find it very doable for me. I basically set a workable goal, like - OK this is what I'm going to test for the next X time period. I always set a specific time period, maybe just for this week and if it goes well, I'm going to try it for two weeks. Or let us say for two weeks I'm going to do twenty push-ups, versus playing games on my phone.

What this does, is instead of focusing at the tactical level, it lets you take it one step above. In other words, you can say that I have all these series of tactics, but instead of just choosing one and guessing that it is going to work, I am going to use a strategy that stays on for one or two weeks. Test this, test that, and so on. Soon enough you will be far more productive when you find a tactic that works.

Take note of what I said, a tactic that works, versus just a tactic you just think will work.

Make clear guidelines.

One of the most important things to do before you start your day every day is to have your to-do list for what's important. Now here is how to do it. Each night before going to bed, think of the three most-priority task that you want to finish. I want you to pick three things that you really want to execute on.

One example is if your work is related to sales. You can spend all day, answering emails and doing all these tasks that are thrown at you, plus other unrelated work tasks. At the end of the day, what's going to matter is going to be those three huge chunks of tasks. You can spend all day doing other things but you will feel more accomplished if you were able to check on those priority tasks.

Focus on prioritizing the important things. If you're running a project for work, it's probably going to be how much time you save, how much money you save, how many clients you serve. If you start to notice that there are other unimportant tasks and there are others you can postpone, you will be able to weed them out.

If in case you cannot move things on the list, you may still have to do it but you may have to deprioritize it. Again at the end of each day you can spend all day answering emails and doing all the tasks but you are going to be measured on finishing what is really important.

These three things to remember can only work if you try to implement it in your everyday work. You already know it for sure, but taking action is really what makes the difference.

STEP 1 - Making an inventory of your skills

The very first thing that you must do, is identify your strengths. Start with the things you already know. If you already know where you excel, then good for you—you have a great head start. It would still be greatly beneficial for you if you do this exercise of listing it down. You might be awkwardly surprised of the things you overlook upon yourself.

Believe it or not, strengths is almost always associated with skills. By the end of this chapter, I encourage you to do an exercise of which I've included a worksheet so you can assess yourself thoroughly, what are the things I am good at, that people will be willing to pay for. Do not make things up! The purpose of this exercise is to really find out where you excel, and from where you excel, comes out your unlimited source of energy. I'm pretty sure you won't get tired of doing it no matter what.

If you're not really good at computers or you say your skills aren't computer related, just list it down. We just need to put everything out on paper at this stage. Remember, we are on the process of making an inventory, so nothing is wrong in this stage.

"But I'm not good at anything!"
"My skills are not in demand."
"I don't think I have enough experience doing this."
"There's a lot of people better than me."
"I don't know what to do."

Listening to this inner voice gets you nowhere. I would suggest now that you ignore all the objections that your brain is telling you. You wouldn't necessarily do something you hate just to make some extra cash because at a certain point you're just going to give up and it's not going to be a good use of your time.

The truth is, you are not really expected to know what you really want to do when you suddenly want to enter freelancing regardless of your age. The good thing though is that every step you take should be getting you closer to what you are passionate about. So unless you absolutely need the money, you shouldn't be doing a job that you really don't like doing.

Time for action. If you are not yet aware which type of job you really must do, I suggest you try to fill this table up. You can write this down on a separate sheet of paper or your mini-notebook.

Fields	Services
Design	Webpage design
	UX design
	Marketing design
Writing	Copywriting for Amazon sellers
	Writing for non-fiction books
	Blog article writing
Programming	Web developing
	Mobile app developing
	Debugging

These are just samples that I have keyed in so you know more or less how you are going to put in inventory the skills that you already have.

If in case you've really tried hard. If you feel like you really don't have a skill you can provide, then it is very ideal that you pick a skill you would like to learn and be good at it. You always have to aim on learning something new. This part is investing in yourself. If you don't, nobody else will.

Investing in Yourself

Not investing in yourself will give you a hard time competing with others. You don't need a degree with learning a new software, that's for sure. There are lots and lots of resources online you can devour to learn. There are tons of free courses online if you will just look around. Nowadays, it is almost a crime to be uneducated, because we are all swimming in a big ocean of information. You just need a few hours each day to learn these, no need for another diploma.

There are free websites to learn, but you cannot learn the full scope, and you will have to do more research. I'd recommend try and pay for these short courses only if you aim to specialize at something. These websites covers mostly the technical stuff, be it programming, design and other computer softwares. Worry not if you don't want to spend additional money just to learn something new. There are tons and tons of tutorials online so it is quite difficult to focus.

I have assembled a list of websites for you to start learning something new. I have categorized it mainly for their features so you know exactly where to search for learning resources. You can find other learning materials on video streaming sites like YouTube and Vimeo but there are too many of them for you to filter. So to save you time on searching, here are the specific ones.

Here are some of the best sites to learn coding and programming. I have included the full address because some of them have really tricky names and it could be hard to find and remember. By the time I am writing this, all of the sites here are still up and running so check them out now.

- ☒ www.codecademy.com
- ☒ www.codeschool.com

- www.udemy.com
- www.codeplace.com
- courses.platzi.com (they have design, business and marketing as well)
- code.org
- www.thinkful.com
- teamtreehouse.com
- www.baserails.com
- onemonth.com

For creatives, you cannot go wrong with this next list. Some of the courses and videos are paid but it will all be worth it. Think of it as an investment for yourself.

- www.creativelive.com
- www.lynda.com
- www.udemy.com
- www.skillshare.com
- www.coursera.org
- www.edx.org
- curious.com
- coursmos.com

If you want to learn a new language, you have to check out these ones below.

- www.duolingo.com
- www.busuu.com
- www.livinglanguage.com
- www.memrise.com

Other mixed courses, guides, science related things and mini courses can be found on these following sites. Some of these may not really relate directly to essential freelancing skills but these are still worth sharing and you might want to check them out.

- ed.ted.com
- www.khanacademy.org
- guides.co
- www.crunchbase.com

Skill List

At some time in your career life, you could have provided some service at work. Here's a quick list of the skills that we can consider on online freelancing. These are not in any particular order so worry not.

- ☒ Web Developing and designing
- ☒ Teaching and Tutoring
- ☒ Photography
- ☒ Sales and Marketing
- ☒ Writing and Copywriting
- ☒ Article/Blog Writing
- ☒ Graphic Design
- ☒ Creative Design
- ☒ Audio/Video Production
- ☒ Interpreting
- ☒ Branding and Public Relations

- ☒ Admin Support and Assistance
- ☒ Customer Service
- ☒ Search Engine Optimization
- ☒ 3D modelling and CAD
- ☒ Game Development
- ☒ Translation
- ☒ Web Researching
- ☒ Legal Services
- ☒ Transcription
- ☒ Data Entry Jobs

You may want to look at the things or services that you are also paying for, that you think you can do yourself. However, do not limit yourself in listing even the smallest things that you know you're good at. A good example could be making a PowerPoint presentation. If you're really good at it, then great! There's a need for that type of service.

Browse other freelancers

If you're already aware of your list and you're still not sure about what to do, check out freelancing websites. What you can do is, search the type of jobs and see which one is being relatively high paying. You may want to compare it with the list you have now. If you think you can do a particular type of skill, make note of it.

Here's an example: A graphic designer is usually assumed as someone who already knows Photoshop, right? But the scope is veeeeery wide, it ranges from doing print designs like flyers and brochures and other materials, to digital ads like animated banners or email banners to social media infographics.

If I were a client who posted a job about a single page, back to back designed flyer, and I just saw two freelancers, one of them specializes in everything, and one of them specifically does flyers and he's been specializing on it, who do you think I would choose to do the job? It is the one good at flyers. Because I want to save time and make sure my job gets done. That's the only thing I need.

What we are trying to achieve here is identifying your niche. This approach is also known as niching down. Narrowing down the options up to the very specific area. You may also call this approach "narrow minded" and that means literally narrowing it down.

You cannot just put your title in that says "Graphic Designer" when there could be 500,000 people who are using the same title. A client will not waste time browsing from lots and lots of repetitive pages of freelancers that look very similar if he can just pick the best one that comes up when searching.

STEP 2 - Finding Your Niche Market

What is a niche?

I am very certain you're raising an eyebrow while reading this part. So in case you did not know a niche is the specific type of service that you would want to be a part of. Graphic designing for example would be too wide for a scope. So going deeper you may find services like doing eBook covers or specializing on flyers and brochures. It is more like specializing on a specific type of task.

Right now you could be wondering why you need to do this market research when in fact you are not really selling anything here, right?

"Do I really need to do this?"
"I am a professional at doing something. I don't need to sell. Eew."

Wrong. If there is one commodity that you are selling, guess what, you are selling not just your skills, not just your expertise, but you're offering them your time. Time is a commodity, right? So with that said, you should, and you should be very careful about how much it costs you every time you sell your time.

So why do market research? Here's an example, let's say you know how you draw sketches of fruits. Let us be more specific, like you know how to draw a mango with your eyes closed. But then, when you look at the job postings, nobody needs that kind of skill. You're in good luck if you find one or two, but then there are other people who are also great at it, and chances are they are also better than you.

See the big picture? If there is a demand, there are customers in it, if there are customers in it, there is definitely money in it. Same goes with you selling your skill online. You should learn to pick your battles. The jobs you search for must match specifically with the set of skills you have, that's true, but you should not forget to consider if there is a demand for that.

Why do market research?

On this portion, we will not be really looking into the market per se, but rather the niche under the market for specificity. By the way, have you heard the old proverb, "A jack of all trades is a master of none."? Exactly. The reason we have to search for that one niche where you truly can grow as a freelancer is the same mindset, as finding where the green grass is.

You then want to ask, "Can I belong to more than one niche?"

It is not necessary to belong in only one niche, but only if you can. You do not want to accept a lot of jobs from different niches and end up not hitting deadlines, or mixing clients' names. Find the balance on where you can do both, but do not overdo it. You know in investment they have this thing called 'diversity'? Nope. It doesn't apply here.

What you should think about is where to put your focus on, and pour out everything you've got. You think you can do great logos by hand? Specialize in logos. You think you can type at a 150wpm with 95% accuracy? Do data entry jobs. You think you can do animations in an hour? Try video production.

There was this time, when I had problems with my android phone, on the charging port. There's just too many technicians to choose where to have it looked at. Most android phones are just the same in structure, yes? But if you have a particular brand, say Samsung and you care about how it gets repaired - Of course, you'll bring it to an authorized repair center.

One word. Specialists. We all love people who specialize at something. If you're putting your efforts thinly and widely spread, you will have a hard time hitting your target. Clients think the same way most of the time. They all want to look for the ones who are expert at what they are doing. You cannot establish yourself as an expert at something if you do not actively think about it.

How do I find my niche?

I do understand it will never be easy for some to find their own niche. I will not feel sorry for you but my goal here is to help you find it. I wish to encourage you more, but I have to give you tough love. A life changing scenario like, waking up tomorrow morning, and then you just suddenly thought you know the answer to yourself - that's not going to happen.

It takes patience, and you have to actively keep looking for it. It will take time for you to be able to find it through lots of experimenting and failing, but once you find it, finding your projects will be a lot easier.

What are the things to look out for?

This part is actually a case to case basis as this may not be applicable to all the clients' job post but it is noteworthy to keep an eye on the small details when you're browsing for jobs.

Of course it is a no brainer to only check out the jobs that you can particularly do and deliver. I won't suggest you doing a type of job that is not really your forte. If the location is outside your timeline, consider the job post if it is time sensitive. Some clients only wish to accept freelancers who are at the same timeline for convenience purposes and ease of communication.

If you can adjust with their times, the better. The downside, you will be on graveyard shift. Remember, you are in control of your time here. It basically depends on your choice.

With that in mind, here are some important points to quickly check out:

- Payment Verified
- Jobs history
- Feedback and ratings

Where can I search?

There are other notable websites you can search for when you're still finding your true self. This is like the soul searching equivalent of finding a job that fits like a glove.

The following are the best I have known so far:

- Upwork
- Toptal
- Freelancer
- Craigslist
- Guru
- 99designs
- Onlinejobs.ph

There are a lot of other websites that I do not wish to include, so as not to overwhelm you while you are searching for your one true love. For now, we will focus on searching jobs with Upwork as they are a front runner with these freelancing websites.

Now the Upwork search engine has a very comprehensive search system for job listings, from the type of jobs you want, price, title of jobs, skills, up to very last exact phrase, you can optimize your search. These websites have already made it easy to look for someone out there who needs you to do the job for them. It eliminates the thought of you going out there trying to sell yourself to people and asking them if they want you to do something for them.

Step 3 - The Profile That Gets You Hired

Here we are my friend. You have finally decided to go for online freelancing jobs. From here begins your journey on moving out of your comfort zone. You are learning that a world exists right inside the four corners of your monitor. Yes, it is another world for you to explore. Your digital workplace begins here.

Get the right profile photo

Photos have been a very important part of our daily digital lives. It is an innate skill for us people to put out our phones and hit that camera app whenever we are about to eat, having a great time with friends, or visiting a scenic view. Of course, we like to get connected.

Even when we're at work, we still like to share things about it. Our work desk, our shoes of the day, outfit of the day, meal of the day, and the list goes on. It is almost always instantaneous for some people that has the itch of sharing things online.

It has never been a chore to do a selfie with most people but when we're doing profiling for our applications and work resumes, it becomes a whole different story. Everything about it should be professional, so let us take a closer look on the must-do things for our profile photo. We will be zooming in on the details because it counts.

Never ignore surroundings

Great background for your profile photo should never be too busy, or noisy. It is very ideal if you have someone to take the few shots for you since not all selfie cameras are top notch. Keep in mind about the location always. It is a no no if there are other people who will be included in the frame. This photo should all be about you and no one else.

If it cannot be helped, a camera feature that blurs the background would greatly help, and adds sophistication too. Pick a place where the surroundings can help you elevate your credibility such as a bookshelf, or your work area, or your desktop/laptop. It pays if you keep them all on the background blurred so all the attention of the viewer gets right on the center of your nose.

Remember natural lights

The word photograph is a combination of two Greek words *phōtos* which means light and *graphé* that means representation of lines, together they mean "drawing with light".

Extreme lighting conditions will not be very helpful. A place with very low lighting would result to underexposure leaving a lot of shadowy parts of your face, and nobody wants to look at that. On the other hand, too much lighting would render your photo overexposed which does not spell nice because most details will be lost.

So why not use flash? Well you can, and no one says you cannot. But professional photographers suggest that there is a massive difference between using a flash and not, giving you a look that is simply impossible to capture with natural light alone. The shift in mood between the natural light photos and the ones in flash feels almost tangible: from bright to dramatic... from a standard outdoor portrait to a cinematic one.

The camera that does the job

"The best camera is the one that is with you." The sentence that is very much popularized by the visionary photographer, director and social artist Chase Jarvis, from his book and has taken the point of views of photography literally to a different level. It simplifies the fact that you really do not need to have a high end piece of camera to do great shots.

Let's face it, not everyone is a real serious photographer, but when it comes to your profile photo for work resume or anything related to your profession, it should beam out that energy of professionalism. A clean, slick and stylish portrait will do, but really, all you have to think about, is that it should represent yourself in visuals that is refreshing to the eyes.

Most of the camera phone nowadays can do great at self-portraits if you just tinker into it. There is no need to have those high pixel cameras but it is great if you have one. If you have a friend who is into photography, use it to your advantage, ask him or her to practice some portraiture shooting. You get what you need, and the photographer adds a new one to the portfolio.

What matters is the composition and the thought you put into while shooting. Keep in mind to put a very nice, warm, inviting smile. If you overdo it, it will look too cheesy. Doing otherwise would give off a weird vibe. You can try experimenting on different angles, and have others look at it. Go take some shots and then buzz your co-worker or someone that you trust to give you an honest feedback. Find about ten of them and then see if you are doing it right.

Pick the right angle

Just because you did a work selfie, doesn't mean to look like your regular selfie. In this case, you should hold your camera at shoulder level, should you face up or down is really up to you but bear in mind not to take things extremely. Remember, this is a selfie for work, not an online dating site.

In framing, before you take that shot, make sure to put your face to the center. Your camera should have that grid lines to help you better, if not, then remember the rule of thirds. This means that you are dividing the frame into three parts and your aim is to keep the center of your face inside that frame on the center.

Consider your clothing

Yes, you can work on your pajamas. Yes, you can work shirtless. You can even work naked if you want but that's a different type of freelancing job.

For profile pictures, that is a totally different story. A profile picture is the digital equivalent of putting your resume picture. You have to take it seriously because you are selling yourself here so you have to package yourself well.

It is not somewhat mandatory to put on business clothes but if you can, that is a great plus. What I recommend is for you to think what would you wear if you were at work at a certain company. Think for example, if you are in a design firm, a white V-neck shirt with a gray hoodie would work. Of course, don't wear the hoodie at work. Think of Mark Zuckerberg. How about this one, dark turtleneck sweaters, blue jeans and a pair of classic New Balance sneakers. Can you guess who? That's right. Steve Jobs.

If you are considering to wear something colorful, make sure it is not really overpowering. Your choice of color reflects on your image, and your personality. Dark colored clothing is usually perceived as dominant, expressing authority and gives out a more formal look. On the other hand, wearing clothes that are light emits a friendly tone and approachable energy. A combination of both bright and dark colors tell people that you are something else. A good contrast of colors suggest a very powerful image in a nice way, so keep in mind what you wear when taking a picture.

I am a graphic designer by profession, so colors matter to me a lot. Here is a list of colors and what they mean when you choose them to accentuate your whole look or when you are picking a theme. This applies too on your resume should you decide to make one that is design oriented.

Now let us look deeper into each and one of them.

Blue. There are a lot of shades of blue, but it is ideal to pick one so as not to make the whole look confusing to the eyes. Navy blue, royal blue and aquamarine blue are good examples. They emit a certain type of energy that is trustworthy, professionalism and reliability. It is said to have great effect when you are having a first meeting with potential clients, or when you are trying to sell a pitch.

Red. You have to be very careful when you pick red as an accent. It is a make or break situation because in some cases, it can be too strong and it could break the whole style you wish to have. This is one of the risky choices you can pick but if you do it well, it can do you wonders.

A simple idea of how to take advantage of red is using it to make people remember you, such as, red framed eyeglasses, or a red scarf. Too much red emits energy of aggressiveness, rebelliousness and is somewhat too bold to the eyes.

On the other hand, if you can effectively use it for your advantage, it is effective in attracting attention and sends out that energy of passion, confidence, authority and success.

Pink. Pink is somewhat close to the shades of red. It is ideal to pick the lightest one that you can so it will not overwhelm the eyes. Pastel colors are the way to go when choosing this shade. It is incredibly effective and a powerful color to bring out that energy of confidence and being in control. There are some notable figures in the business world that uses the same principle of color picking. Warren Buffet, Bill Clinton and Donald Trump are a few of these men that are often seen wearing these colors on a regular basis.

This shade of color is ideal when you are into public speaking, doing presentations or if you want to imbibe some sense of influence to people that you wish to associate with.

Purple. If you combine both blue and shades of pink, you got purple. In a similar way, purple emits a combination of professionalism and passion. A lighter shade or a darker one both sends out a type of energy that is that speaks of control, power and confidence.

Purple is also easy on the eyes as it can be either feminine or masculine. It is one of those neutral colors that can be used to take advantage of different situations such as attending interviews or when dealing with females. It speaks that energy of being approachable and not overwhelming.

In some ways, it is almost always effective to combine purple with more shades of blue, or light pink. Always remember though not to use more than two shades of color at a time.

Green. Dark green always implies growth and wealth. It is the general color that comes in mind when you think of money. In the corporate world, it is associated with selling and influencing people as well. In the real world, feel free to wear this color when you wish to attend meetings or doing a video conference. There is always this inviting, organic feeling when you pick dark shades of green, and it is also recommended to use it to accentuate your whole look, such as your business tie, or pocket square. Always think of choosing colors that are complementary.

Light green on the other hand sends out an aura of serenity and calmness. It is inviting to the eye as well when you wish to land on your new proposals and get hired. It is fresh for the eyes and it is worth remembering when clients tend to browse a lot of profiles when they are searching.

Yellow. While it may come as too strong or overpowering, choosing yellow to combine with the other dark colored choices will help complement each other. It sends out vibrant energy and optimism, but it is not really reliable by itself. Choose this route if you aim to put some contrast in your clothing. Yellow shades is best paired with dark shades of blue, or black.

In any case, stay away from too much bright yellow. You can pick ones with just a hint of it such as beige or dirty white. Again, keep in mind pastel colors! If you cannot help but include yellow, always put in mind to use it discreetly.

Orange. Tangerine is ideal when using it as accents, but not by using it on itself alone. It is best paired with shades of blue as it complements each other very effectively. This shade of color is very attention grabbing and it gives a great impression to the eyes.

Black. Black is as elegant as white if you use it well as a complementary or base color. It fits on most occasions, setting and situation. It is the color that signifies professionalism, sophistication, and it gives out a great impression on style, plus it is timeless. You will not have a hard time combining black and using any of the colors listed above as accent.

Optimize your title

Let us now tackle one of the most important part of your profile which lets you get searched more frequently. This is not the cure-all for your whole profile but consider it as your core concept. With your tagline, you are basically going to want to come up with a unique set of words. I definitely would not copy exactly what everyone else is doing here but you can consider what others are doing so you will see which one works and which does not.

The professional title and skill tag section appears at the top of your profile. Now if you have not submitted your profile yet you will see a screen when you log in that is prompting you to complete your profile, so go ahead and click on the big green button that says 'complete my profile'.

Once your profile has been approved you can actually go into job listings and click on the names of other freelancers that have applied for those jobs and see how they have the profile setup that can be very helpful or that can also be very encouraging to see how incompetent your competition is but for now we don't have access to those jobs so I recommend putting two to three keywords that describe what you do. For me I do mainly eBook designs, Content Marketing designs and Createspace formatting. I chose to pick those words because I have done my own research on my niche and found out that these types of small projects are the ones I can do on my free hours, and at the same time, it has a very reasonable amount of pay. Information products is the thing of the future so I know people are willing to pay for it. It is something I know that I can do for a certain amount of time, at a consistent pace.

You have a little over 60 characters here so you could list what makes sense but you don't have to go too crazy with it now if you have only one primary area of interest that you can describe for your title you may want to describe what makes you different from your competition. For example if you design logos you could put "Minimalist Logo Design" or "Reliable and Fast Logo Design," that one is a bit cheesy but you get the idea. Actually you can just give a hint of what makes you different than your competition, so you stand out when you appear in the search results. Never try to put the same keywords that everyone else is using or else, you're like a needle in a haystack.

Put relevant skills on profile

Move on to skill tags. They are actually optional but I would recommend you go ahead and fill them in. This is important since it is used when people are searching for freelancers and it also gives potential clients a quick snapshot of what your skill set is before even clicking on your profile now you can add up to 10 skills and you want to add as many skills as possible for a full listing of all the skills that you can add.

Upwork allows you to browse freelancers by skill and just to give you an idea if you don't really know what to put - there are over 2700 different skills so you have no reason to tell me you cannot put something in there. I would recommend that you have maxed out the skills tag of up to ten. In the future, you may notice that you are keen in getting jobs that are in a related field but not precisely described in your professional title or your skill tags, so if that's the case you could always go back and change them to fit your skill set. Always remember to consider the relevancy of each skill tag you use.

Write a description that never gets ignored

When you look at the overview, it is like your job description when you are filling up your resume. Always think of your profile contents as what you would put inside your curriculum vitae. In online freelancing, the overview or the description works the same way.

Crafting your overview is a very important part of your profile because when a client clicks on your profile this is most likely the very first thing they're going to be reading. Surely, this really can make or break the hiring. So what makes a great overview? There actually has been a lot of different styles of overviews, some of them work really well some of them don't work at all.

But I'm going to show you the formula that's worked really well for me so first I recommend starting out with a fairly short intro that summarizes what you do. Squeeze in one or two sentences first, in your own words about your personality. Take note, that clients are people too, and they want to work with somebody they like.

You can put just a couple of sentences talking about yourself and a very brief overview of the things that you do. Next thing to do is list out all the various job types that you are willing to take on. Doing this actually allows clients to scan your profile and get a good idea of what you offer. You might want to start with a very short list of what you can do and then extend that list over time. It is a good practice to take a look at this list about once a month and make sure that everything there is accurate and make sure that if you've found another lucrative job category, I suggest you include that in.

To give you an example, before I did book designs, I was just working on the cover designs, because I found out that there is a huge market and people need good cover designs. I did not offer mine cheap, but I make sure I am offering quality and value. So then I found out that doing book layout and formatting is also in demand, and it is something that I can do fast and easily, so then after I realize that moment, I decided to add it onto my title and overview and that has helped me out immensely. There's been multiple occasions where clients have actually reached out to me after seeing my profile and I've landed a job to formatting a kiddie book for Createspace.

What I have found out is that no matter what you do with your profile contents, eventually you will find little niches that you probably haven't even thought of yet and you will want to add that to your profile as you go along.

It is a good idea to add a little note telling potential clients how to contact you. You can also give them a guarantee that you'll respond within 12 hours. People are a lot more likely to ask you questions if they know they'll get a quick response and questions almost always lead to jobs so you want to make sure that potential clients feel comfortable asking, and for them not to hesitate to reach out.

The about me section is just a very short bio and this is about reminding your clients that you're a real person with a life outside of Upwork you can put where you live and maybe what you enjoy doing with your free time whatever you can think of and try to show a little personality here, like if you're doing a podcast, or a book author, or if you have a blog that is appropriate for work, or just an entertaining one.

Lastly, you can put a few of your best reviews. Ideally the best one would work, but maximized at three. Some people find it effective to put it at the very beginning of your overview section of your profile or at the bottom. Either way works in my opinion and it's a matter of preference. See which one feels better for you. The purpose of this is just about social proof which gives a long way towards building trust.

Now I know that since you are just starting out you won't have any reviews from Upwork clients but if you have any other reviews from other sites you could add them here or you can wait until you get your first glowing review from a client and then go ahead and post it.

That is it for your overview and please take your time designing your overview as this part can really make-or-break a deal and you need to make sure that you do a really good job.

BONUS TIP: What I recommend also that is worth doing is copy other people's overview. And by this, I do not mean literally copy every word because you will get in trouble for sure. Just take the ones you need that you think fits you well, and then reconstruct it, interpret it through your words; make it your own. Make adjustments so you know if you want to use the ones you like to copy and kind of switch it up and put in some of your own wording and sentences. Be safe.

Setting up your pricing and rate

Whether you're an article or designing a webpage you have to have an hourly rate. Everything takes at least one or two hours to make. Your rate will change over the course of time.

For example my hourly rate used to be $5. And over the course of time, as I gain great reviews from one-time projects and clients that are coming back, I was able to raise my rate to $10, $15, and now, my rate is $30 per hour.

It is basically how much value you want to put on yourself. What you do, and what you know? Let's apply this to how I do eBook cover designs. I just had to figure out how many designs I can make in one hour and I can do two of them quickly with all the details provided like title, main title, and the author. I researched and figured that an effective book cover always have these three elements. The graphics are only add-ons to engage the interest of the customer. I then decided that vector designs is the easiest route I can go with since there is no need to download other images or graphics.

When it comes a time that the book topic is just a hard one, and a design concept rarely flows, I steal ideas from other best sellers and I make my own version. There is no limit to what you can do with vectors. That is why I fell in love with doing vector designs.

If you observe other freelancers on their rates and pricing, you can use it to test the waters. Someone else may have a lower price or a higher price depending on what value they give themselves and their time. That is how you come up with a starting point for your work and after that you can adjust the price based on how well you do.

If you are able to deliver projects very quickly and you're leaving a smile on each client's face then you know you need to raise your price. It's that simple.

If you are charging rates that are too low, you will devalue yourself because you will only attract the clients that are not valuing quality work. Clients like these are usually the source of many complains. If you apply the 20:80 principle. 20% of your paying clients are usually the source of 80% of the income you get. So my suggestion is, find more clients that belong to the 20% and you can start refusing those that you do not like. Give them an offer that could be unacceptable to them, but do not be rude. Stay nice to them.

Now here's what happens when you undercharge. This is not a new concept but it is very applicable on every type of job in freelancing. I learned this concept with Danny Margulies which is a freelance copywriter. He compares this loophole to driving so fast down the highway, that you don't have time to stop and tune-up the engine of the car.

Low Hourly Rate → Working Crazy Hours → Little Available Time → Repeat

Start charging low rates and you will need to work more and burn yourself out and you end up with not a lot of time available for online courses, learning your craft, learning your trade, networking with other freelancers, learning the best practices. You are just trapped. You are just working all the time and it will be hard to break-out from it.

How to include a video profile

Video profiles will become one of the most important employment tools for job seekers and employing companies in the future. It is a great tool for them to see if you as a candidate inspires them or fit with the culture of their company before they study the qualifications on your resume. In some cases there are tens of persons submitting a proposal and it is quite a good advantage if you have a video profile at your disposal.

Before you start making your video profile ask yourself what makes up your brand. Ask yourself—what are your values, work ethic, and passion. How would you describe yourself in a business setting? Are you introverted or extroverted? Soloist or a team player?

To keep things simple, you should be mindful of these three things so to keep your video profile short and concise.

- ☒ Who you are
- ☒ What you do (Be very specific)
- ☒ Whom do you work with

These are all important questions to ask yourself before you start making your video profile. It should be full of content but needs to be shortened and kept with the meatiest parts. Remember, this should be no longer than a minute. Make sure you close with a strong straightforward statement.

If you have not already watched the movie The Intern, well you should. It is a great movie. There is that part where Robert deNiro is making a video resume. Try to check that one out and get ideas from there. It is a short but thoughtfully made video resume that he did for his internship job.

Taking Relevant Tests

For some people, taking the tests is just one way of measuring their lifetime knowledge about things that they learned from the past, and oh do they love the challenge and they love putting out those trophies. Some are not-a-fan of this part. But for the sake of completion of the profile, we should take the tests. Notice that I did not say "you have to," but it is recommended. The take tests section amplifies the skill tags that you have included earlier in such a way that it validates whether you really know about the subjects or not.

In the profile section you are going to want to scroll all the way to the bottom down and see the test section and what you can basically see there is the current test you've taken, the score that you got, and the time it took you to complete it. And whether you want to display publicly your test results or not is completely up to you.

Ideally, you should only display the results of the ones that are above average. If you can manage to be better at each, then please do so. Taking a particular test gives you a whole wide range of different tests that Upwork provides. It is a great medium to prove your skills and impress potential clients by taking the free tests. The more relevant tests you pass, the more professional your profile look.

Read the test policies and rules before starting any test. Make sure to set aside a particular amount of time to finish the test. Keep in mind that they have a scoring algorithm here so try to reach for the perfect score if you can. It is not a problem however if you do not make it on the first try because you can try again and re-take the test. Same goes if you want to keep taking the test until you get a higher score. You cannot expect though that the same questions will be asked so it cannot always guarantee a higher score the next time you take it. If you fail the test then you actually have to wait a certain set amount of time before you can retake it I believe it's either like a day or two here it is no penalty for failing a skill set test you can take as many as you want you have to wait 30 days so which is actually quite a long while.

The percentile rankings work in terms of where you rank among all the test takers. Ideally, you would want to belong to the above average, but of course, if you can do better and be on the top percentage of test takers, it is a huge plus.

There is no problem being completely honest about taking the test but if you think you can open another tab and do a Google search for the questions while taking exams, you might be able to find some answers. I don't necessarily condone cheating but then again these are like some of those tests where it's like some of the questions are just so specific which urges you to do that little cheating. Nothing's wrong with it, because in the end, you learned something from it, and you passed a question, which is a win-win situation. Whether you cheat or not is entirely up to you.

I would recommend to take the basic tests, you can see how many have taken a particular test. The higher the number of tests taken, means it is more likely a must take, or one that is highly recommended. A good example for this is the "US Basic English Test." Ultimately, the more of these tests you take and pass with flying colors, the better chances of you getting more job invites.

Building a portfolio

One of the most common question that is asked: What do I put into my portfolio? So you're probably starting off right now and you're looking to get some work and you're going online trying to figure out what you're supposed to put into your portfolio. You're probably finding tips like you got to include your best work and have different types of medium and you're probably thinking to yourself, "How is that supposed to help me?"

All right let me break this down for you. So think about this: Why would anyone go out of their way to look at your portfolio or to look at your website to look at your different pieces of work? It is because they're looking to hire someone like you, right? And the reason why they're looking at any of your work is because they are looking for some sort of proof that you can provide the benefit that they are looking for.

You have to figure out what you want to put into your portfolio. But first, you want to figure out who is looking at your portfolio or rather who your target audience is who wants to hire you.

These people are part of the niche that you determine first when you decide on the market you wish to serve. You have to find out who exactly these people are. You want to find out their needs and their problems and the benefits that they're looking for. Once you discover the benefits, then you can go back and reverse engineer this in a way and you can put together the portfolio that demonstrate your skills. Understand their needs and their wants first and if it demonstrates that you have what they need, they will see you as an expert and they will trust in your work.

The internet is your opportunity to build a platform first, whether it's YouTube, a blog, a podcast. You must develop a way to invest in something for your audience before they ever invest in you. This applies with accomplishing a very well curated portfolio of your past projects or achievements. Why? Because clients are into seeing results. They want proof to see that you are the one they need.

Now for some actionable tips. Portfolios are somewhat a tangible thing that comes in mind, whether in digital form or not. Often than not, it is the type of creative jobs that require you to have samples of work. Now if you are one of those that does not have any finished project yet, you can start by doing just a part of something that is big. I call this the "Movie Trailer" method.

You watch movies, right? So you know these video clips you see online, on TV or somewhere else, and do you know what is the main purpose of it? It is to get you hooked. That is their sales pitch. The movie trailer is the taste test. If you are impressed with the trailer, there is a big chance that you will buy that ticket to the movie premiere.

The same goes with your portfolio. If you do not have something big to show, just do a small part. An example would be a website design. You really do not have to make five different pages, one is enough. Put out everything you can on that one page. If the customer wants to have a sales page, do just one part of it. If a client wants a video to be edited, you can ask them to make a 5-10 second sample. If in case you don't get the job, that's okay. You have a new item on your portfolio. You still win.

Writers can do sample works as well. Creative writers can write small articles that can be up to 300-400 words. You have to check out first and see what topics they wish to have. An example would be a client that wants a blog article about ten tourist spots in Italy. You do not need to write the full article to show them that you can. Give them something to read for about three tourist spots in Italy. Load it on google docs, and then share the link with them when you write the proposal. I am certain it won't take long to write, but then if you don't get the job, it is still okay. You have a new item for your writing portfolio.

For programmers or coders, you do not need to do a huge system, waste time and tire yourself. You can still show off your coding skills by doing small chunks of codes that is relevant to what the client needs. Offer or suggest a direct solution to their problem so you can get their attention.

STEP 4 - Writing Proposals and Selling Yourself

The proposal is your gateway to getting hired by your client. It is often your first introduction to a potential client and the beginning of a new business relationship. So many people tend to mess this up and end up getting ignored. Let's get to it.

I'll be sharing with you three tips on writing a proposal tips we've heard from other freelancers who regularly succeed in getting new clients. We are breaking them down into three important parts.

- ☒ Customize the content
- ☒ Showcase relevant experience
- ☒ Suggest an interview

Customize every proposal. Read each work description carefully and write a customized proposal. Begin with a warm professional greeting. Stand out by explaining how you would complete their project based on what you know from the described work. If something is unclear make sure you ask questions so you know if you have the skills the client is looking for. Attempt only to do the copy-and-paste method if and only if you have made a very similar and specifically detailed proposal before which you think perfectly matches the new client. Be careful though with the names you address. I once have mistaken a "Fernando" with a "Jonathan" due to the same nature of projects that I did with them. I was lucky enough and I cheerfully talked my way out of it and ended up closing another deal.

Make the proposal and sales pitch relevant. Write a short paragraph explaining your relevant experience including your work experience, education and skills. Mention any past jobs you've completed that are similar to this project and prior positions you held that give you the skills the client is looking for. Answer any screening questions the client asks in their work description.

Suggesting an interview. Let the client know your availability for an interview and that you'd like to discuss the project further. Interviewing with a client lets you further establish the trust and rapport you both need to get great results on a project. Keep all payments for your project on the platform so you're sure to get paid for your great work. The wonderful thing here is that if the client feels your core skills and work history match their needs, they'll contact you and you will have them as a recurring client, which builds a good reputation for you and your client as well.

Techniques to win Contracts

I would like to reveal some of the principles of bidding that have worked for me in this competitive, really competitive, marketplace to put together a pretty good side income or part-time income as a freelance designer. These principles are not only applicable to Upwork as you can also use them with other hiring platforms.

Just bid. Like, a lot of it. The first principle is you need to get into a habit of bidding. I know when you get busy on other things it's hard to sit down and actually get around to bidding on things and you need to bid on everything. Pick a time or multiple times during the day when all you do for 20 minutes or half an hour just to look through the listings. Of course bidding on anything costs you two connects per proposal.

There are free proposals—that is only if you get an invitation to interview. If you get an invitation and it looks like a good job—definitely bid on it because they're already high on you. They're already interested in you. If you find that you're running out of connects, and you probably will if you have a free account, go ahead and buy a few more, do a few more bids, or be a little bit more selective in what you're doing but you should be maxing out those connects every month. I consider the cost of using connects as simply the cost of doing business. so you will easily pay for those extra connects or if you have an account you pay for twenty dollars a month, you'll pay for that if you're getting any number of jobs.

Time-sensitive or not? Another important point is to keep on the lookout for time-sensitive jobs. So many clients want jobs done fast, and you'll only see these if you're looking every day or multiple times per day at those listings. These jobs can be really good paying jobs. They can also be dangerous because you have to maybe rush things a bit. Just be careful and see how long the job actually is. Is it 500 pages in 24 hours? No way! Don't do that. You'll only get a bad rating, they might not even pay you. But if somebody wants a really simple design, go ahead—do it.

It is only you who can measure yourself if you can do it fast. So if you can do that in 24, 48 hours, the money can be easy because clients know that you rushed. They'll pay for that rush. Make it sure though that you can deliver, or else, you are just digging your own grave.

Be ready to fail. The next reality of bidding is simply that you're going to fail a lot and just expect that you're going to fail. Don't covet a job before you win it. Don't think, "Wow, there's a one-thousand-dollar job, and I'm bidding on it, I want to get it." Just let it go, forget about it because chances are you going to fail. I think my bidding success rate is about ten percent but I bid on a lot of jobs so I might bid on 30, 40 jobs in a month and get three to four of those jobs. That's pretty good.

So do a lot of bidding, and when you do, you'll win a few of those. If it's a thousand-dollar job—that one job you win that whole month—that's really good. And if you bid on a bunch of smaller jobs, so $50 jobs, $80 jobs, $100 jobs, who knows maybe you win five or six of them and you have a nice 300 to 400 dollar income each month and it doesn't take you that long to do that kind of work.

Bid and then forget about it. My philosophy is to bid on everything and bid and forget, just forget about it, move on, just constantly bid on things and sometimes you'll be surprised. A month later a client comes to you and says "I finally made my decision, I want to choose you." and it's a nice surprise.

Mind your pricing. Another principle of this marketplace is that pricing matters. Now that sounds obvious, but it can be used as a strategy, and simply what I'm saying is despite me having a high rating on the site, I have a 92% quality rating, I still lose out to people who underbid me. So they put in a lower bid price. I've seen people with almost no experience on the site beat me by under bidding me on the contract. I've had clients tell me they really like my profile, they like my ratings, my reviews, but I cost too much.

So lowering your price will always get you some number of clients. You just have to decide how low you're willing to go. A final point on bidding principles that I want to mention is really look out for badly written ads. So if the ad has a lot of mistakes in it, there's a good chance the client may not be worth your time. It sounds harsh, yes. But you do not want to waste time here. You are here to utilize your remaining free time and make extra money.

STEP 5 - Keeping the Wheels Turning

Keeping your clients happy

It is not a secret that maintaining client relationships can be challenging. We have all been there, and it is easy to get frustrated trying to figure out how to keep your clients happy. You might even wonder why these relationships are so crucial to your freelance career. Well, it is actually quite simple: happy clients will spread the word and grow your freelance career in ways that no amount of marketing dollars can match. This is why maintaining a good standing for your rating and ranking is very crucial.

Tell you what—the good news is that nowadays, online freelancers are able to maintain longstanding relationships with clients that can increase loyalty to their brand and in turn, result in more money spent with their company. I will be sharing with you five basic ways to engage more with your clients.

1. Be a good listener.
Always be willing to listen to new ideas, comments, and especially criticism from your clients. For better or worse, your clients are going to share their opinions. So, you may as well hear it straight from them. And, more importantly, if you take the time to respond to negative feedback, it will show how much you care about the customer experience.

2. Give them a great review or a feedback.
You can only do this if they really, really deserve it. It always helps to know that your clients have reviews too that are publicly posted in exchange to a feedback they gave you. It gives them a credibility boost, and it helps them to have a bit of yourself as a freelancer, it is a good way to get remembered. People who will read your response will be impressed that you took the time to put a short but meaningful review because they are deserving to get it.

3. Always have a desired goal to your interaction.

Whether it's to increase sales, client loyalty, or resolve client concerns, having a desired outcome will constantly improve your freelance career. In other words, every interaction with your client should offer value to them, while building your reputation at the same time.

4. Make it personal.

I know it's a business for you, but your clients don't have to feel that way. If you personalize the client experience, you build a stronger business relationship.

Any way you can involve your clients on a more personal level makes them feel more like a friend than just a paying customer. It would be wise to know a few things about their culture if you are from a different part of the world. Send them a sincere greeting on holidays or ask them about a hobby or talk about something that is outside the scope of work. Small talk can do wonders if you execute it nicely.

5. Always provide impeccable customer service.

You can definitely pull ahead of the competition with this one. Who hasn't been turned off by a brand who dropped the ball with their customer service?

Whether you have a helpdesk with a live chat feature, 24/7 customer service, or a fast email turnaround, the service provider that replies promptly to customer concerns is the one people stick with for the long haul. A freelancer must provide an online experience which parallels real world experience in order to satisfy their clients. A brand needs to have this type of positive give and take with their clients to be successful.

Not only will these clients remain loyal to a brand they can trust, but they will help grow your business. That is right. This freelancer-client relationship is what is over the strong foundation of trust.

How to attract high paying clients

This is probably one of the most common question you hear from freelancers of different platforms is this: "How can I attract high-paying clients?"

Well, if you have not figured it out by now, those elusive dream clients are not shopping at your local market or the ninety-nine cent store and they are definitely not shopping around the internet for weeks just searching out your cheapest competitor.

They want the best, they want it now, and they are willing to pay for it. So, if you want to attract your higher paying clients, here is how to do it.

1. Raise your prices.

You should not actually overthink about this one. Just raise your prices. That is it. Raise your prices. Now personally, I have been able to sell $20 to $250 packages in cover and book designing, and I still look for ways that I can increase my own prices. And if you are one of the serious individuals with a serious inquiry into how you can actually attract those higher paying clients, I would like to propose that perhaps you are not really interested in learning some secret elusive formula, although those are always nice, but rather you are simply looking for permission.

It is the permission to raise your prices and charge more. If that is the case, well, permission granted. You see, telling you to raise your prices is one thing, but actually doing it, it takes guts. It could be really scary. You see our brains are wired to think, "If I raise my prices, I increase my risk of getting the 'NO' and if I get the 'NO', well then it just proves I am not worth it— I hate rejection. And in case you are not aware, we all do too.

And that is not just the case at all. You see, it has become common knowledge that a higher price attracts a higher quality customer, right? And that is what we all want at the end of the day. Those dream clients and students that remind us of why we are doing what we decided to do in the first place.

2. Understand what the client wants, and give it to them.

So here are some broad stroke generalizations that we can all agree on that a higher paying client or customer really resembles.

- They have money. And they are not afraid to spend it on the things they want and need.
- They know time is valuable. You can be sure that they do not waste it.
- They take responsibility for their lives; they do not play victim to it.
- They take action and then they get results.

So even though you and I could be in completely different industries or fields, we can both agree that offering our coaching, services, or products at a premium price must deliver something that:

1. Saves precious time for your client,
2. Focuses on high level activities or topics that yield lasting results for them.

Even if the simple act of raising your prices will attract a higher paying audience, you may also need to tweak or adjust your offer. Just because one of your strategy worked with one client, does not mean it will work with them all.

Now that the elusive secret has been revealed to you, you have a choice to make. Do you continue to undervalue yourself and charge low prices that not only attract clients that make you pull your hair out but also keep you scrambling to find that next one so you can pay the bills? Or do you take that extremely brave and daring leap to raise your prices and attract your dream clients?

If you have a commitment to providing extraordinary service to your clients, I give you full permission to raise your prices and go forth confidently into the market place.

Under-promising and Over-delivering

If you want to have a massive change with your freelancing career, you better under promise. As it also goes with doing business, it should always be a goal to make all clients happy. But for me that would be not enough. Settling for an okay-type-of-job is good but making it exceptionally great is what clients really want because they get more than what they pay for.

If you know you're going to deliver on Thursday, well you should tell them to expect delivery Friday. You could be asking, "Hey, isn't that lying?" Yes! But you bought yourself enough room if you did mess up on Thursday and you had to get it to them on Friday. Now guess what, it is still okay.

When people are demanding your time, you are like a printer—you can only handle five jobs on the press but you have twenty-five requests. What are you going to do? How are you going to meet all these expectations? There's just a flood of things coming at you. It feels like you are in a hornet's nest.

Here is a tool that will help you get out of this dilemma. Here is a boundary that you can set that will really be effective. Instead of over-promising and under-delivering, why don't we work on under promising and over delivering?

Let me show you how to do this. You see, what your clients really expect from you is quality. They really don't want speed. Therefore they are willing to trade speed for some quality.

"Mr. Smith, I realize that you're going to need that done by tomorrow and I am prepared to do that for you, but I know that your primary aim is to get high quality from me and I would like to do that. I would like to get this done by Thursday at four o'clock—or how about Friday at five o'clock? You will have the best darn job. You're really going to get what you're paying for. You're going to get the value that you should expect from me."

Mr. Smith says, "Absolutely, I would rather have the quality instead of the speed."

Always negotiate speed with higher quality, right? Under-promise and over-deliver and then schedule it out in your calendar because you do not know what is going to come up. You create allowance for all those serendipitous things that may come up in between. You might have to take care of them and then you schedule it for Friday but you will get it done by Thursday.

So now you are showing that you are getting it done faster. Under-promise and over-deliver. Surprise them. Excite people by doing more. In reality, when we under-promise and over-deliver we can really wow people because at the end of the day it is all about the client's expectations. Start thinking about what are the possibilities of how you can under promise and over deliver so people will love what you do, and they do not feel just "okay" with what you do.

Conclusion

No exercise equipment can get you fit if you do not use it. No book that promises change can get you to higher learning if you read it but do not practice it. The same goes with teachings that are not applied and advices that are not heed. Speaking of giving advice, I have learned that there are actually three types of people. You may have heard it somewhere before, and yes! It is in the bible. Check out The Parable of the Sower. Only for this part I am comparing it with these three types.

- People who do not listen to any advice. These are the ones who want to do things their way. They do not listen with the intention of understanding. They only listen with the intention of replying.
- People who listen, and think that the advice makes sense, but does not take action. These are the ones that always make excuses. These are the ones who tend to delay actions with every reasoning they find.
- People who listen, analyze and examine the advice in intricate detail so to find that it makes perfect sense. They take action, and embrace change.

So which one are you?

I do hope the ideas and tips I have presented here can induce more success in your freelance career if you already have one. If you are planning, beginning and experimenting to try it, I wish you success. The only way to find out is to try it. You can reject everything I have taught in here, or simply accept it. Tweak it, turn it into something better. The choice is all yours.

If you find yourself in a situation where getting your first job is a catch-22, accept the fact though that failing is part of it all. But don not just fail. Fail smart. If you think you are going to fail... fail fast and try again. That is the only way to achieving success. No one has ever done it from zero to success without failing. Failing is part of the process.

I would like to wrap this up by leaving with you a quote from John Maxwell that applies to us freelancers on the way we relate to clients which also applies on business and entrepreneurship

He said, "People don't care how much you know until they know how much you care." If you take care of them, they will take care of you.

www.ingramcontent.com/pod-product-compliance
Lightning Source LLC
Chambersburg PA
CBHW070133230526
45472CB00004B/1519